j994
R393a

ROIT PUBLIC LIBRARY

DETROIT PUBLIC LIBRARY

W9-CPL-497

DETROIT PUBLIC LIBRARY

KNAPP BRANCH LIBRARY
13330 CONANT, DETROIT, MI 48212
852-4283

DATE DUE

BC-3

JUL 99

KN-j

Published by Creative Education
123 South Broad Street, Mankato, Minnesota 56001
Creative Education is an imprint of The Creative Company

Designed by Stephanie Blumenthal
Production Design by Patricia Bickner Linder

Photographs by: FPG International, International Stock, Peter Arnold, Inc.,
and Tom Stack & Associates

Copyright © 1999 Creative Education.
International copyrights reserved in all countries.
No part of this book may be reproduced in any form without
written permission from the publisher.

Library of Congress Cataloging-in-Publication Data

Richardson, Adele, 1966–
Australia / by Adele Richardson
p. cm. — (Let's Investigate)
Includes glossary.
Summary: An introduction to the only country that is also a continent,
describing its geography, history, wildlife, government, culture, and places to visit.
ISBN 0-88682-341-2
1. Australia—Juvenile literature.   [1. Australia.]
I. Title.   II. Series: Let's investigate (Mankato, Minn.)
DU96.R53   1999
994—dc21   97-4997

First edition

2 4 6 8 9 7 5 3 1

AUSTRALIA

ADELE RICHARDSON

Creative Education

AUSTRALIA

F A C T

Australia is nick-named "the land down under" because it lies entirely in the southern hemi-sphere; it's almost halfway around the world from England, its mother country.

Above, laughing kook-aburra; right, koala

When you think of Australia, you may think of kanga-roos and fuzzy koalas, or friendly people with cheerful accents saying, "G'Day, Mate!" But Australia is much more than that. With its rich history and unique wildlife, Australia is a place like no other.

The coastline (including Tasmania) is about 22,800 miles (36,708 km) long. That's nearly the same size as the United States, minus Alaska and Hawaii.

5

LAND AND CLIMATE

Australia's official name is the Commonwealth of Australia. It is the world's smallest **continent,** and at the same time, the world's sixth largest country.

Left, olive sea snake; below, Australia's flag

AUSTRALIA

BIG

Australia is the only country in the world to occupy an entire continent by itself.

AUSTRALIA

WEATHER

The state of New South Wales is home to both the hottest and coldest places in Australia.

Right, evening at the Sydney Opera House

The country is made up of six states—five mainland, meaning in the main part of the country, and the island of Tasmania. The five mainland states are New South Wales, Victoria, Queensland, Western Australia, and South Australia. There are also two **federal territories** on the mainland, the Northern Territory and the Australian Capital Territory, where Canberra, the capital of the country is located.

O ver 86 per-
cent of all
Australians
live in coastal areas
because the interior of
the country is so dry and
harsh. This interior is
known as "the outback."
The most populated
areas of the country are
the east, southeast, and
southwest coasts.

AUSTRALIA
DANGER

Shark attacks have happened so often that the most populated beaches have fenced-in sections so people can swim in safety.

7

Below, great white sharks are powerful ocean predators

AUSTRALIA
F A C T

In 1788, an English penal colony, or prison, was set up in what is now Sydney, Australia; 161,000 prisoners lived there.

Above, a pair of sulphur-crested cockatoos; right, Pinnacles Desert

Australia is a very dry land with many deserts. Its lakes, which may look large on a map, are usually nothing more than dry salt and clay basins. The largest salt lake is Lake Eyre, which covers about 3,700 square miles (9,583 sq km) of land. This lake holds water only about twice every 100 years, when unusually heavy amounts of rain fall. The rest of the time the little water that reaches it quickly evaporates, or dries up.

As a result, most of the time there is nothing but a crust of salt on the ground. Aside from all the desert land, the country also has thousands of acres of pasture and farming land. Some of the most important crops that are grown are wheat, sugarcane, and potatoes.

AUSTRALIA
FACT

Apart from Antarctica, Australia is the driest continent in the world, with 11 major deserts.

AUSTRALIA
BIRDS

Some Australian cockatoos will travel together in flocks of 1,000 or more.

9

AUSTRALIA
DOCTORS

Every state and territory has a base set up for the Royal Flying Doctor Service. These doctors travel by airplane to visit sick people in far away places.

Right, Cradle Mountain and Dove Lake, on the island of Tasmania

Overall, Australia has no "general" **climate.** One-third of the country can reach temperatures of over 100 degrees Fahrenheit (38°C). At the same time, another area may be covered in snow. Most of Australia does not receive much rainfall, and in some places droughts, or shortages of water, can happen every season.

Kids who live in the outback have no transportation to school; they must listen to the radio to get their assignments and mail their work to be graded.

Left, surfing is a popular sport; below, a pair of red-collared lorikeets

AUSTRALIA OPPOSITES

Because it is in the **southern hemisphere,** there are a few "opposites" that happen in Australia. For example, the further north you travel, the warmer the temperature becomes. The summer months are December through February, and many Australians spend their Christmas vacation playing on warm beaches. The winter months are June through August.

In the **northern hemisphere** hurricanes and tornadoes spin in a clockwise direction, or to the right. But south of the equator, where Australia lies, these storms are called anticyclones because they spin in the opposite direction, or to the left.

AUSTRALIA
F A C T

Because of the harsh climate, the water in most Australian lakes evaporates very quickly.

AUSTRALIA
I S L A N D

In 1642 Abel Tasman landed on the south shore of an island that was later named after him—Tasmania.

Top right, Kakadu National Park, Northern Territory; bottom right, cliffsides of ancient fossilized coral reef, Geikie Gorge National Park

HISTORY AND GROWTH

Ancient European geographers did not know exactly where, or how big, Australia was, so they labeled the area on early maps as *Terra Australis Incognita,* which means "the unknown south land." No one really knows who the first European was to actually see Australia. It is known that the Dutch were the first to explore the west and north coasts of the country. They called the unknown country New Holland.

Captain James Cook reached Australia on April 29, 1770, aboard the Endeavour. He claimed the eastern part of the continent for England and named it New South Wales. England established a penal colony, or prison, at Botany Bay in 1787. They sent 11 ships carrying about 1,500 people to the new land.

There are more than 120 different species of marsupials on the continent.

Left, banana tree; above, agile wallaby

14

AUSTRALIA
MOUNTAIN

Australia's highest point is Mount Kosciusko at 7,130 feet (2,173 m), which is small compared to North America's highest point—Mount McKinley—at 20,320 feet (6,193 m).

Right, sheep farms are common in Australia

Eventually, more English colonists came to Australia. These settlers claimed land and began farming wheat and raising sheep, cattle, and pigs.

The Chinese also came to Australia. But the Europeans started the "White Australia" policy, which kept non-white people from moving there.

This policy stayed in effect until 1972. Today there are more than 17 million people from many different cultures living in Australia.

AUSTRALIA
F A C T

Australia is the world's oldest continent. Some scientists believe that it is more than one billion years old.

Above, a meteor crater

AUSTRALIA
LAND

More than two-thirds of the entire continent is desert or semidesert.

AUSTRALIA
FACT

Seventy-five percent of Australians own their own home—that's one of the highest percentages of home-ownership in the world.

Right, dingoes; far right, Aboriginal child

THE ABORIGINES

Exceptions to the "White Australia" policy were the **Aborigines.** This race of dark-skinned people were already in the new land when the Europeans settled.

The Aborigines formed **tribes** and became a group of wandering hunters and food-gatherers. Because of this, territory was very important to them. They often set up tribal boundaries marked by trees, rocks, and billabongs (water holes).

AUSTRALIA
LAW

The law says that people who are able to vote must do so; if they don't, they may have to pay a fine.

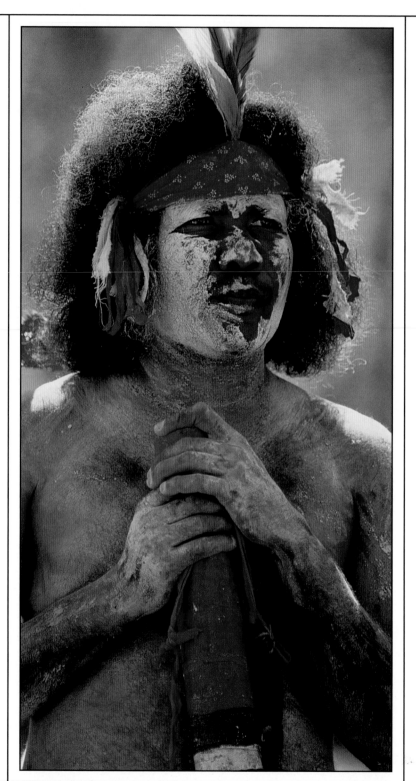

An Aborigine

Aborigines were very skillful hunters. Spears and boomerangs were their most important weapons. The Aborigines used two kinds of boomerangs. One is the kind that returns to the hunter after it is thrown. This weapon is made of hardwood and is bent almost into the shape of the letter "L."

One side is completely flat. The other is raised, or slightly rounded. This was used to drive flocks of birds into nets.

The other kind of boomerang is non-returning. It was used mainly for fighting and hunting.

The ancient Aborigines painted the walls of caves and made rock carvings depicting their way of life. Much of this art still exists. Today all Aborigines are Australian citizens, but they hold on to many of the traditions of their culture.

Cape Barren goose with young

AUSTRALIA
F A C T

Australia is the lowest continent in the world with only six percent of its surface higher than 2,000 feet (609 m) above sea level.

AUSTRALIA
BIG BIRD

The emu can grow to weigh as much as 120 pounds (54 kg).

Above, an emu with nest; right, Melbourne

AUSTRALIA LAW

Over time, the country has developed three levels of **government.** The highest is the federal, or Commonwealth, government. It is responsible for any matters that affect the whole country, such as trading with other countries and controlling how many people move into Australia. The head of this government is the king or queen of England. There are also six state governments and more than 900 local governments.

Australia is a **democratic** country, which means the people choose their leaders through elections. The elections process is a very serious matter in Australia. In fact, all Australian citizens who are 18 years old or over must vote.

AUSTRALIA
SPEED

The red kangaroo can travel at speeds of up to 30 miles per hour (48 kph).

Above, young sheep are sometimes bottle fed

Because of the country's English tradition, the Australian flag is decorated with a small copy of England's flag, called the Union Jack. This represents the Australian government's early ties to England. A large seven-pointed Commonwealth star is below the Union Jack. This represents the six states and the territories. There are also five more stars which represent the **constellation** Southern Cross, a star cluster that can be seen only in the southern hemisphere.

AUSTRALIA
F A C T

Australia has a very high literacy rate; 99.5 percent of the population can read and write.

23

WONDERFUL WILDLIFE

Some of the best known animals in Australia are its **marsupials,** animals that have pouches to feed and carry their young. One such marsupial is the red kangaroo, which is pictured on the Australian coat of arms. The male has a reddish-brown colored coat. Most people would think the female is the same color, but she's not! Her coat is gray.

Far left: pink cocka-too; left: a pair of red kangaroos

AUSTRALIA
SETTLERS

By 1830 more than half the Europeans in Australia were people who had spent time in England's jails.

Another marsupial is the **koala** bear. The koala has gray fur and looks like a little bear with big, fluffy ears. It lives along the eastern coast of Australia and is a legally protected species. The animal eats the leaves of **eucalyptus** and gum trees. Other marsupials include wallabies (small relatives of the kangaroo), possums, wombats, and the Tasmanian devil.

Right, koala mother and young; far right; an emu

J ust as famous as Australia's marsupials are its birds. There are more than 700 species of birds on the continent. One unusual bird is the **emu.** It is the second largest bird in the world (behind the ostrich) and can grow to be up to six feet tall. The emu cannot fly because it has short wings.

AUSTRALIA
F A C T

The koala eats up to two and one-half pounds (1.1 kg) of leaves a day; its favorite food is eucalyptus leaves.

AUSTRALIA

Some anthropologists believe the Aborigines lived in Australia more than 30,000 years ago. This would make them the oldest race on earth today.

26

AUSTRALIA

Flag symbols are placed on a red flag background for merchant ships registered in Australia.

Right, black swans; far right; parrots

The black swan (which is the state symbol of Western Australia) is native to the continent along with 55 species of parrots, such as the cockatoo, parakeet, and lorikeet. Many of Australia's birds are brightly colored and beautiful to look at. As a result, some people steal the birds and sneak them out of the country.

MYTH

The Tasmanian devil is only a cartoon character.

FACT

The Tasmanian devil really exists. It's a ferocious dog-like marsupial that comes out at night to find food.

28

Above, young Tasmanian devils; right, Ayers Rock

VISITING AUSTRALIA

Millions of people choose to visit Australia. The country is unique and offers many places of interest. One such place is Ayers Rock, the world's largest **monolith.** This red sandstone wonder stands 1,143 feet (348 m) above the desert floor in Central Australia.

Another popular tour site is the Sydney Opera House, one of the most unusual buildings in the world.

AUSTRALIA
ISLANDS

Australia owns the Coral Sea Islands, which are very small (only a few square miles of land); no one lives on the islands except for the wildlife.

AUSTRALIA
GAMES

Football, the most popular sport in Australia, is played on an oval field with 18 men on each team.

Some people visit the Great Barrier Reef off the northeast coast. The reef is the largest **coral** structure in the world. Its length is 1,245 miles (2,000 km) from Cape York to Brisbane. It contains 350 species of coral and is a favorite spot for diving and snorkeling.

Top right, the Great Barrier Reef; bottom right, pink anemonefish

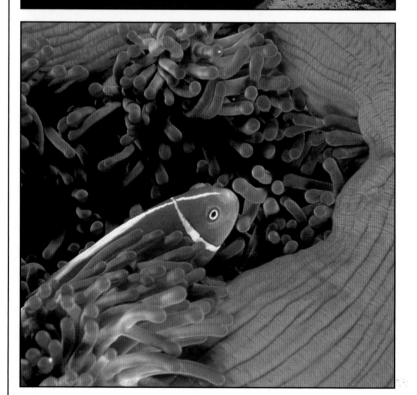

Whatever a visitor's interest, Australia is sure to have something special to do or see. From its vast desert regions to its snowy mountains, Australia is the most diverse continent in the world. Its people are very friendly, and the animals are like no others in the world. It's easy to see why millions of people from around the world take an interest in "the land down under."

Red Centre desert

The koala rarely takes a drink of water; its name comes from an Aboriginal word for "seldom drinks."

Glossary

The **Aborigines** (ab-uh-RIJ-in-eez) are a race of dark-skinned people native to Australia.

An area's **climate** is the average type of weather determined over several years.

Land was often claimed and developed by people, or **colonists,** moving there from another land.

A **constellation** is a group of stars that can be connected by imaginary lines to make a picture in the sky.

A **continent** is any one of the seven large divisions of land on the earth.

Coral is the outer skeletons of tiny sea animals.

A **democratic** system gives the power of government to the people through free elections and voting.

Dingoes are a species of wild dog found only in Australia.

An **emu** (EE-moo) is a tall bird, similar to an ostrich, that doesn't fly.

A **eucalyptus** (yoo-kuh-LIP-tis) is an Australian evergreen tree.

Federal territories are areas of land that a government owns.

Geographers are specialists who study the earth.

A nation's **government** controls and directs the laws and rules of a nation.

A **koala** is a marsupial native to Australia; it is about two feet long (61 cm) with sharp claws and large, fluffy ears.

A **marsupial** is any kind of animal that has a pouch to feed and carry its young.

A huge stone or structure is often called a **monolith.**

The **northern hemisphere** is the half of the earth that is above the equator.

The **southern hemisphere** is the half of the earth that is below the equator.

Tribes are small groups of people who share the same beliefs and interests.